PROJECTION AND PROPAGANDA

A BRIEF TREATMENT

Tarl Warwick
2017

COPYRIGHT AND DISCLAIMER

PREFACE

The essential premise of this work is to remind people that generally speaking they have been either lied to or at the very least misled regarding politicians, pundits, and others. Instead of packing this text with page after page of meaningless filler I'd rather keep it short and sweet for the purpose of my audience, which is intelligent enough not to need a hundred pages of fluffed up content.

Appearance and perception trump reality and objectivity nearly 100% of the time. We'd love to believe this isn't true and that the "facts" we hear and the images we see are iron-clad and totally beyond any debate; this is an illusion largely fed to use by politicians, pundits, religious leaders, and many others within society which use these false objective means to project the illusions they wish us to endorse so that they can control us or at least influence us. I will vaccinate you against these practices here and attempt to do my very best to open your mind to inoculate it against such assaults on your senses.

Few things are objective; it is objective that things evolve, and this has a meaning within politics and religion- once you defang these zealots and political talking heads by recognizing them for what they are it is much easier to judge and deflect their words, easier to accept or decline their messages. Through this process a more intelligent population is created.

PROJECTION AND PROPAGANDA

PROJECTIVE IMAGE: MAKING A STRONG MAN FROM AN OLD MAN

When we view politicians debating on a public stage, the vast majority of those watching them become mesmerized after a fashion and fall in line into the all-too-common habit of taking ignoring reality and any outside stimuli and fixating on which politician out of the two (usually two) is "better." Two politicians with fundamentally similar platforms may be differentiated because of some manufactured political issue of no considerable substance or importance at all because much of their worldview is identical or nearly so.

We can find no greater example of this manifest propaganda than the 2016 presidential election in the United States: The three major figures of the entire race were all over 65, one was almost 75. They were, nonetheless, envisioned by their fans as being strong and capable of leadership. In few realms would we imagine it was a good idea to take someone who may drop dead of a stroke at any random time the helm of great importance unless they had some truly stellar aspects to their characters. Fans of these various candidates may look askance to this remark; I don't provide it for a political reason (I am looking past politics itself per se) but for the purposes of illustrating the hilarity of the image. Also included in the eclectic mix of candidates who received substantial vote shares were another older lady who vandalized a bulldozer and a man who gave an interview in which he broke down into baby talk in an attempt to show how effortless it would be to win a debate against the two major candidates left standing after the primaries.

PROJECTION AND PROPAGANDA

Projection and charisma (as well as propaganda in the literary or any other sense) can make a person perceive reality in such a drastically different way from its more true "objective" form with such great ease that it is almost pointless to mention reality to most people so long as they have any emotion invested in something. Walk up to someone who is madly in love with someone else who will never date them, or who is actually a total asshole several steps below the afflicted party. Now try to convince them "this is a bad idea"- I am only joking, you shouldn't actually do that, because they're more likely to punch you in the neck than to actually change their mind.

Emotion is a funny thing; so useful, but sometimes so purely useless. In a perfect world people would suspend it at least long enough to realize they're lied to on a daily basis; the ads they see all lie by omission, if not in worse ways, regularly. The political speeches they deem of such soaring quality are often riddled with errors, hype, emotional appeals, and every fallacy under the sun. The pundits on the news that they digest mentally like bowls of gruel are just reading a script concocted by people with a fiscal, social, and political ax to grind (nearly one hundred percent of the time.) Even off script, they can get caught out lying in the most spectacular of ways- sometimes they even get fired because of it, but don't worry, it's just an "isolated incident" when it happens!

You, the reader, have been lied to more times in your life, than you have been told the truth. Some of these lies are good and even come from your staunchest supporters; they're there to keep your emotional state intact. If you knew how many times your food sucked, your clothes were disgusting, what you said was dumb, and you weren't told because it wasn't meaningful enough for anyone to interject, you'd cringe. Yes, even those of you who are highly intelligent, attractive, skilled, or powerful. That is the first truth.

OFTEN THOSE IN HIGH POSITION ARE PHYSICALLY NORMAL OR EVEN LOWER

Makeup is a lovely thing. So are proper lighting systems, echoing microphones, and all the other trappings of convincing a group of people that a fundamentally normal or even below-average individual is worth casting a vote for, donating to, or listening to on the news because they become (via magic of course) more honest by looking "good."

This is not a trick merely used by politicians and pundits; most celebrities cake the makeup on, and some of them get plastic surgery. We often mistake this for an attempt (in a vacuum) to "look young" because of their own desire to have a good self image when they look in the mirror. Nonsense- more often it's to market themselves more effectively. Even those who are quite attractive age in due time, and while some people age quite well, others (who wish to compete with those lucky few) modify themselves quite often, to retain that little bit of edge.

Take off the makeup and a lot of those politicians and pundits look normal- those scar-free faces on the news at night are not exactly pristine.

This is essentially propaganda; "listen to us, we're the beautiful ones." Hollywood does it, pundits and politicians do it- look at ads you see regularly on billboards, television, the internet; have you ever seen anyone on one that representes a product that isn't without blemish and perfectly lit? Simple projection- a charisma and sparkle that is nearly totally artificial. It is not a lie per se, merely an illusory sort of persona that associates with what is to be sold; an object, a service, a bit of punditry and analysis, etc.

PROJECTION AND PROPAGANDA

Sometimes those who arise to high stations are not even quite normal and would generally be considered below average on the scale of desirability. Richard Nixon was noted for his heavy use of makeup, and overdid it during televised debates with his far younger opponent, none other than JFK himself (who was considered to be highly attractive- but that too was projection, he was simply being compared to people at least a decade or two older, favorably.)

There is an additional effect here which is not propaganda in and of itself (or even dishonest but natural)- power projection becomes much easier when a person is flanked by others. Put a crowd of fifty thousand people in front of an otherwise powerless, mortal man, and he begins to look quite intimidating and charismatic indeed unless he is verbally impotent. This arises commonly in political situations, musical concerts, and so forth; less so with punditry where the crowd is not gathered together in one place.

This is still an illusion. Properly recorded or broadcast, sweeping footage of large crowds during political rallies can give a sort of shine to people who are at best average, or even below that; people who make merely decent speeches are seen as more charismatic, people who are only decent looking shine like gods as they gesture for applause and seem to magically command the masses before them, parting the seas of people like Moses as they walk to the podium to deliver a speech that was not even written by them.

ASSOCIATIONS USED TO INFLUENCE

Those who wish to project power can easily do so by association, all the world is indeed a stage, and their theatrical behavior can be surprisingly like reading a Shakespearean play at times, replete with all of its intrigue, which of course is not always completely real; sometimes its projection! There are different associations, all of which are fairly archetypal, used to project a little bit of extra character that sometimes a boring politician or pundit does not actually have; their stronger, more real associations are often related to their legendary rates of alcoholism and extra-marital affairs.

Male politicians especially seem to have a twofold dynamic where extremely stereotypical roles are played by one or more (but usually only one of each) individuals in their inner circle. Observe the interactions between former president of the United States, Obama, and vice president Joe Biden. The "bromance" spoken of between them by the media was probably half manufactured, although they did seem to have a genuine relationship that went beyond the cameras- the current president, Donald Trump, seems to have a similar dynamic with multiple people, who he has surrounded himself with, only to cut them lose or repeatedly change their stature within his administration through selectively demoting them from the limelight.

This first role is filled by jesters in the modern sense; these additional male figures are less dominant and typically less physically imposing by some standard or another. Often, they seem to be older as well, or physically less attractive. These individuals exist, in the strictest sense, to be compared with the major partner in the arrangement, kind of like a younger, less well spoken, but still adept co-host on a television or radio show. The same basic dynamic is assuredly at play. The subjugated individual can also serve as a sort of ideological whipping boy (or girl, at times) in order to distract the ire of some audience or another from any problems with the dominant partner.

At least once in living history this master-and-minion situation was abandoned and flipped upside down; namely, the 2008 US election. John McCain's running mate, Sarah Palin, was arguably more aggressive and outgoing than him for some time, and was spoken of as having "gone rogue." Some of this might have been theatrical, as sometimes is the case- it could have well been a sort of attempt to drag more female voters on board by creating a "strong, independent woman leading an older man into the new century" approach. It could also be that his running mate actually began to ignore his marching orders, without repercussion because it was too late in the game for him to even consider switching her out for a different vice presidential would-be.

So then we have the jesters- but sometimes someone more physically or verbally commanding is needed, perhaps to soften the image of the politician, pundit, or other figure, or possibly in a situational way. Presidents love to stand next to war-worn, weathered military commanders with gruff "commanding" voices, and shake their hands firmly as the flag waves nearby. Behold, the nightly news likes to have "experts" on which they allow far more leeway in interrupting and ranting than they do some other guests- the news anchor, the pundit, may largely stand by in awe and let nature take its course because this dominant partner, situationally, is giving their program a little extra shine. Here you have your knights (or you may term them wingmen)- they can be utilized to improve physical appearance or merely to project a sort of charismatic stature. The US government unknowingly helps to create a stronger image of all major political candidates simply by flanking them with secret service members who look like spies ready to infiltrate a UFO base with lasers and jetpacks.

Males will also often flank themselves with attractive females; this is a fairly long-standing tradition, and amounts to a modern day (although voluntary, usually) "concubine" of sorts. The female candidate or pundit will often flank themselves with highly athletic men (temple guards you may term them) as part of the same general class of activity. In either case something is being projected; the male is projecting essentially his mating capabilities by being in proximity to females that many men would not be able to closely approach, showing his dominance. The female is doing the same, by surrounding herself with one or more males who are physically strong, potent, and fit. Simple psychology in action in order to project an image that may well be totally false; either the male or female may be physically worn down and disgusting behind pancake makeup, but they are still projecting power. The Queen of England does this all the time. She's feeble, but she has enough firepower traveling around with her to conquer a small country, and that is enough to dissuade anyone from challenging her supremacy.

A fake group dynamic can also be crafted in which multiple equals form together and make the pretense of a close relationship in order to project a sort of friendly collegiate image for others to see, like when groups of senators stand on stage and shake hands and deliver what amounts to a sermon; in reality some of the people on stage almost surely detest one another, sleep with one anothers' spouses (or staff, or kids, or parents), or something of that kind, but the image of teamwork is important because of what they are supposed to be doing for a living.

SHIFTING TOPICS, ARTIFICIAL IMPORTANCE

Often times one of the most potent manners within which to confuse an opponent is to shift topics. This variant of propaganda is so common that it has become virtually hegemonic within modern political discourse- issues that have very little true relevance have been built up into relevant conversational topics (sometimes of a quite heated, emotional manner) over time, or were injected more forcefully and suddenly. The US debate over gay marriage took decades to play out and for about a decade was of secondary importance only because political (and public) will was so against bringing it up when able to avoid the same. The European debate over immigration was, at first, completely ignored with the justification that opposing the anti-sovereignty status quo was "racist" and then over the course of only a couple of years went from a niche and fringe issue laughed at but discussed, to now possibly the top issue of most European nations, because it has become entirely conflated with and paired with the European question of post-nationalism.

These issues though became important largely because of public will- what about those that would never be considered relevant by any significant total thereof were it not for the manipulation of others? Some hard hitting front-page news stories of the last presidential election included a fly buzzing around Hillary Clinton's head and how Donald Trump enjoyed his steak. John Kasich's food habits were also up for public debate. An entire book could probably be written about the issue of Marco Rubio's debate breakdown.

No sane politician will attempt to force an issue into

public discourse where the population by and large does not agree with them- they will however harp on something repeatedly and attempt to make it more of a popular discussion topic. Martin O'Malley did this repeatedly in the last US election; he mentioned his green energy plan many times, each time falling flat, but it was an issue that, had it been on more minds among the left, he probably would have gained massively on- a decade ago he might have been likened to a younger Al Gore and become the nominee.

O'Malley failed. Others succeeded. Never since the days of the Irish Potato Famine has immigration been so front and center and so singularly so for so long in a presidential campaign; but this was the issue Donald Trump could win on, so he slammed away single-mindedly, to the astonishment of most of the pundit class, that declared he would inevitably falter and die out as a candidate when the public stopped talking about his apparent one-issue platform. That probably would have happened, except that he made sure to force himself into the news on a daily basis by insulting others- a strategy that won him no fans in DC and many fans on main street.

These are just a small number of examples from a single election- but the same concept happens time and time again; climate change was once a major issue in politics, now you hear relatively less about it. It was an artificially important topic too since a casual view of the evidence given shows us that if climate change is a threat, and exists, humans will not be capable of reversing it- it will either solve itself via a feedback mechanism or it will inevitably cause so much havoc the entire world order collapses into chaos. By shrouding science in morality both the "deniers" and those who accepted the principle of anthropic climate change sparred for years. Was anything done? As far as significant policies, did anything change? One would think it odd that after twenty years of nonstop alarmism, no substantial steps had been taken to ward off a doomsday that was approaching within a single generation- the pessimistic proponents of the entire concept muttered unhappily about governments dragging their heels or being genocidally stupid, but it's more an issue of the issue losing its luster over time as it was talked into the ground- once it lost importance, the politicians who know full well the concept is either false or we're all doomed began to ignore it because it was no longer profitable to speak about it. A few fringe individuals like Bernie Sanders continue to ramble about the need for governments "to do more" without fundamentally understanding what he's saying.

Modern politics is such a Shakespearean farce that you could artificially limit conversation to whether or not a society ought to ban paper plates. On its own, if I suggested this to a crowd of people, most of them would laugh and the rest worry for my sanity. If I combine the suggested ban with the explanation that the plates "contribute to global warming" or "are usually made in regimes that have poor human rights records" or "are inefficient and we should use ceramic because it can be reused many times at lower overall cost" suddenly my ridiculous suggestion will take root in some of the minds beholding it. Hysterically, once I have mesmerized the audience, after a fashion, into this discourse, it would take someone more charismatic and orally skilled to sway them away from my central fallacy (that only a ban can solve these largely unrelated side issues I used to justify my retarded suggestion) into common sense, where some other, more sane discussion can be had.

POLITICIANS A REPRESENTATIVE SAMPLE OF POPULATION, OFTEN

In an autocratic system where there is a genetic lineage of power (either recognized or de facto, IE a dictator passing the reigns to their child or kin) the leader may have relatively little in common with the people "represented" by their leadership- indeed the family may be part of a genetically distinct minority that holds power specifically because long ago it subjugated the majority cultural bloc.

In a system where representation is codified though the vices and virtues of the leadership tend to generally reflect if not a majority of the population, at least a decent chunk of the same. When a politician is corrupt, we tend to reflect upon it as though a substantial number of regular people wouldn't act in the same manner; they would, which is why every form of government of necessity will experience scandals, problems, and difficulties internally and externally. There can never be a perfected government, just a stable system. The issues at hand at any given time may be misrepresented in their importance by a politician for personal and political gain but the issue would not be useful for this purpose if a large number of people weren't at least *capable* of experiencing strong opinions about the same.

That poses perhaps the greatest risk over time to this entire world, at least if we focus on human causes of destruction instead of those involving nature which are less predictable; when people ask why we fight in wars, the answer is biological, for the mental (and its offshoots) are just an extension of innate evolution within behavior- war is just the logical, technologically enhanced extension of chimpanzee fighting- and chimpanzees will attack members sometimes without any cause whatsoever, singularly or in groups. They threaten, attack, and berate neighboring chimpanzee clans, they mock and injure their own members for reasons not even at this time fully understood but which must involve access to resources. Even this is remarkably close to human behavior- we do the same things.

The worst human tendencies are actually innate. There is no human being in this world today who does not at least occasionally think of doing violence to others, often in a manner others would find unjustified. There are no humans alive today who have lived for very long who haven't fantasized about waging war in some form, about killing. These tendencies though are buried deep and seldom expressed because of laws and social norms repressing mans' violent tendencies. A thousand years ago so long as you externalized the violence to another tribe or chiefdom it was not only acceptable but was commendable in the eyes of leader and slave alike. When we realize that even genocide, as an extension of war and our even more apelike former behaviors, we can better understand two things; why the world is violent and "messed up" (at least according to most people) and why we occasionally see "abnormal" people who commit atrocities; has anyone bothered to ask why so many obviously psychotic, unstable people find their way into power? They become warmongering tyrants, or bloodied revolutionaries, or cult leaders- why? Because they help others express their own bottled rage and make it doctrinal, dogmatic, and acceptable to do so. This always leads to bloodshed, even though rarely the tyrannical, bloodthirsty charismatic may be in a "proper" role and thus highly useful. Alexander the Great was fundamentally a non-reformist interested only in conquest, but happened to exist at the right time to spread "civilized" ideas to the East leaving behind smaller but nonetheless important cultural enclaves and technology.

PROJECTION AND PROPAGANDA

So the violent, psychotic cult leader is merely more open about the kind of views others have but do not express. For every pervert who acts on their perversions a great many others "only fantasize" about the same- but those people, were they not repressed culturally or legally, would act on them in a more "real" sense.

The insane tyrant is little different from a power mad alpha chimpanzee. The same tyrant is also not far removed from a well-remembered conqueror of antiquity- a great Caesar perhaps, or a victorious, long-lived, battle hardened king. The history of the development of mankind is pockmarked by episodes of the most extreme violence, and at no significant number of times did the "normal" and "peace loving" people think to stop these tyrants and kings and cult leaders. Most often they either fled or obeyed. The "normal" people who did not wish to take part in battle were pleased when standardized, conscripted militaries were invented- not because it exonerated them from fighting physically, but because it created a new artificial category of human beings to blame for war- the soldiers and officers, upon which they, as jingoists, externalized their own warmongering. Inevitably- and the world has nuclear weapons in it which is highly pertinent to this point- a power mad tyrant will rise to power in just the right way to unleash the third world war. It can be staved off, and there are probably groups dedicated solely to this, but those fail-safe systems only have to fail one time to cripple the entire world. That is, in some instances, you can be successful as many times as you want, but it only takes one failure to end your ability to continue- the world of mankind, because of the technology we now have, is essentially one big game of Russian Roulette.

SHAPESHIFTER, WEREWOLF, METHOD ACTOR; METAPHORS FOR THE MASTERS OF REALITY

The proper metaphors for the most talented commanders and leaders are threefold; the werewolf, the shapeshifter, the method actor. In all three cases we have a being with the ability to shift itself, the way it is perceived. A method actor can temporarily suspend their own psyche and project the image of one who is entirely different, and do so with enough talent that others will believe the projection. A werewolf transforms in the literal, visual sense- the metaphor stands, although in many tales the werewolf is an unwilling participant in this moonlit wardrobe changing ceremony. The shapeshifter in the native sense is essentially doing the same but in a voluntary manner.

The true command figure has to possess self control, and that is the ironic key to controlling others; the mundane politician or pundit has enough charisma to fool some people, block them from realizing any non-earth shattering corruption on their part, shine themselves up a bit and make them look more intelligent than they really are. Any decently intelligent human is able to accomplish this.

But to truly control and command requires absolute self control, and any lapse in the same won't do. Should the method actor break character the mesmeric spell is broken and the audience, for a moment, realizes that they are not what they appear. Many leaders are destroyed by scandal because they lacked the ability to hold themselves back from embezzling money, seeking extra-marital affairs, and the like. Their lack of self control leads to a lack of ability to control others, because very soon they fall out of favor and lose their position entirely.

PROJECTION AND PROPAGANDA

In the sense of the Shakespearean thus the more skilled politicians live a public life which is partially scripted and acted, and not genuine at all. We see this in multiple cultures. The pundit pretends to be outraged morally after years and years of reading a teleprompter, and has to at least be half believable in their attempt. The politicians of any legislative body ultimately have more in common with one another than their own constituents (being of course employed in the same manner and place, all of them receiving significant amounts of money for being so) and they have to spend a great deal of time pretending this is not the case. Thus, for the cameras, they will bicker and argue and harangue, but at the end of their short Shakespearean work day they may return to drinking with those same people, who after all tend to be friendly to them.

That is not to say there is not genuine hurt, anger, and so forth, or genuine outrage, among the pundits and politicians. The war general who never lets his troops see him frown and worry, might frown and worry a lot in his tent as his enemies bear down around them all, waiting to destroy his entire army, but in the more public roles of power, much is a farce, little is a truth, and after all, the politician is not employed to tell the truth anyways, but to represent what they feel to be best; sometimes, this will inevitably lead them to lie. The pundit, even when attempting to encourage views they actually believe in, will sometimes be led to ignore reality in order to do so, thinking it pragmatic.

THE BENEVOLENCE OF LEADERS IS NO MORE ADVANCED THAN THAT OF A REGULAR PERSON

One thing that people must understand is that if one cares at all about intent and not just outcome the benevolence (and indeed malevolence) of a leader, one with power, is no different than many within the general population.

A murderous civilian can take a firearm and kill a dozen people. A murderous high level general or politician can have thousands killed or more. A benevolent civilian can rescue a puppy, but the benevolent leader can probably rescue a million of them.

That is, the central, mental characteristics and even intent can be the same, but because the leader has access to greater funding and backing the job (for good or ill) is easier. It is also more likely that more people will hear more often about the evil or good done, because chances are the attention given to the leaders' behavior is greater or less according to that same increase of ability. If the behavior is negative it is likely that attempts will be made to hide it; that gets into a whole different realm of propaganda- as far as the mainstream media (connected to the political elite in all nations and controlled by it outright in the more totalitarian ones) is concerned, the greatest way to cover for a corrupt political figure is to merely not report on the event or events they wish to hide. Lately, the mainstream media has attempted to label anyone not doing so "fake news" and, since that has not worked, now they are trying to use their wealth and assumed "moral authority" to force technology firms to censor such independent figures directly.

PROJECTION AND PROPAGANDA

There is also a more insidious methodology employed from time to time; one that various government agencies are known for. It is hysterically funny that the same people who recognize (based partially on open admission and declassified materials no less in the wake of the collapse of the USSR) that foreign intelligence services and foreign states routinely character assassinate independent media figures and activists, and which elbow in on their media apparatus to suppress some stories and push others into greater circulation, persist in labeling the same claim aimed at US intelligence services as a conspiracy theory- so too do people (usually fans of the establishment) in every other nation. "Of course we don't manipulate you" said the Soviet KGB when it was in full operation, "but those damn Americans are always making propaganda."

Sometimes suppression of reality involves literal cold blooded murder. This last resort is always spoken of by the fringe of independent media as though it was both common and considered the prime method of control; it isn't, because if you employ de facto mind control on someone you don't need to kill them for being problematic. More common is the injection (via controlled opposition) of false narratives using so-called independent individuals who have been bought and paid for and which receive enormous amounts of support from governments, corporations, and the like. Again as before, when one suggests that a person has been bribed by a corporation nobody resists the idea. Now say that a government (especially if they don't oppose the current government in charge) has done so and prepare to be labeled "crazy." In the wake of enormous government ineptitude false narratives involving more sinister motives are quite often pushed onto the investigatory fringe in order to distract them. This certainly happened in the wake of the invasion of Iraq.

GUILT BY ASSOCIATION

Mostly people do not notice propaganda when it has been deployed since it is structured specifically to escape detection. Any attempt to notify people that their mind is being twirled around like a chunk of spaghetti on a fork is met with what has become known as "fluoride stare" (it should be noted that mostly this term is not used by those who believe in a conspiracy to enslave mankind through pumping the water systems full of fluoride and is a running joke.) Sadly, for many people their brainwashing is so complete they will never abandon their (woefully inaccurate) view of reality even if faced with a life or death situation requiring they abandon it.

Multiple narratives we have spoken of; those are sometimes the most interesting because it entails government agencies spreading negative rumors about themselves in order to escape repercussions for actual scandal. Also of use, though, is simple association. In old advertisements you will often see positive associations within products used to sell them; for example the attractive woman is flirting inaudibly with the man who wears some style of clothing or is consuming some sort of tobacco or alcohol. Because they are, on a behavioral level, outdated badly, we can look at ads from roughly the mid 1990s and on back and chuckle at them (and in some years this threshold will encompass later and later waves of ads too- "modern" can never actually exist.) Most people though because of their mental training (brainwashing) cannot intellectually aim this same satire at ads which are modern.

It is the negative side of association that concerns us, however, when speaking of power structures which exist outside of the largely fiscal concerns of the routine, invariably greedy corporate structures of mainstream ads.

PROJECTION AND PROPAGANDA

Since I am explicitly mentioned in the article I can, legally speaking, mention it here; a "news" organization (remember, the media is a power structure) entitled "Right Wing Watch" crafted an article not long before the manufacture of this booklet which claims me to be an enabler of nazis and the far right (despite never having considered myself even a conservative in my life) because I am willing to speak with individuals they have labeled as such (also inaccurate in several cases within their article) and because I have never explicitly "denounced ethnonationalism." This is humorous since it pretends I have some sort of official or codified, dogmatic power and that my disavowal or acceptance is necessary on significant topics; but my content relates mostly to current events and to occultism, not to philosophy.

In the case of this article the fundamental claim is that while I am not myself "bad" (by their standards- and it does attempt to insult me in an underhanded way via its ethnonationalist denunciation reference- which is its own propaganda tactic!) that I am bad nonetheless because I do not directly and publicly hamper the people that this organization considers to be "extremists." Now, since these individuals are unwilling to speak with them, and I am willing to do so, I will trust my judgment of their character more than that of a rich, corporate entity designed predominantly to disseminate propaganda as any other. Importantly, though, this is a tactic deployed often in order to try to grind down the rising independent media. It is also deployed against upstart political fronts (although they are more commonly subjected to mere dismissal- IE "this party/group is too small and thus should not be voted for/supported, because (insert artificially important issue here) is too important to dick around with non-viable movements."

I will briefly describe the side-swipe style of attack so

often used by the old guard media now towards the rising new media.

It goes hand in hand with guilt by association for only when there are things to associate can it be accomplished. If I write an article about someone that is defamatory I can get into monumental legal and potentially financial trouble for it. That wouldn't be good- but I can associate them with something highly negative and then proceed to insinuate that they have at least a loose connection to the same because they have failed to denounce it explicitly. Should they choose to denounce it explicitly as a reaction it makes them look "weak" and if they do not, it can be used as evidence they support said negative movement, person, or idea. This is fairly simplistic since almost no person in history has had a penchant for denouncing everything they dislike, and because through one or two degrees of separation even seeming opposites can be overlapped to a decent degree.

This is vaguely like the five degrees of Hitler game- a slightly amusing trick where, it is said, any randomly chosen article on Wikipedia can be linked to the article about Adolf Hitler taking five links or less. One trick is to get to Germany or World War Two somehow within three clicks, then it's a no-brainer.

The truth is that those who should be doing the explicit denouncing are those who have spent a half century making millions of dollars spewing propaganda, and public officials whose legislative and executive decisions can actually harm other people in a legal sense. Since nobody in the alternative media has such a power, it is hardly our responsibility, and we remain private citizens.

SOME COUNTER PROPAGANDA

Once you recognize something to be a false reality it is fairly easy to dismiss it, the main problem we have on this token is that the population is flooded with multiple kinds of propaganda constantly; even to the point of chaos, since foreign states will be injecting it alongside whatever domestic power structures exist. As communication becomes cheaper and more widespread, the only thing preventing total sensory overload with propaganda is that it gets watered down to a substantial degree by the ability of a billion actual individuals to create independent material. In this way one of the greater defenses of a states' own stability is its populations ready and constant access to the internet and any other pertinent technology, in as uncensored a form as possible.

It has been (incorrectly) stated by some- the New York Times itself made this mistake recently in one of its articles- that censorship and policing on social media creates greater stability over time by blocking some propaganda- this is not actually true. In the short (think the next decade) term perhaps, but as material becomes more and more advanced, common, accessible, and the near-totality of information becomes more and more able to provide more and more opinions of different natures to a greater and greater audience, the use of mere state outlets or state-tolerated and corporate outlets (think, cable news, where five companies control it all) will become utterly vestigial. These formerly powerful edifices in a vaguely capitalist system will go out of business altogether due to inefficiency. In centralized systems they will be unable to create enough material to both entertain and inform and flood out the propaganda. Propaganda itself in the standard sense may die out as well because it is unable to find enough of an audience to justify deploying it in the standard manner.

PROJECTION AND PROPAGANDA

I have written and spoken on the topic of attempting to maintain a free and open internet, with as little censorship as possible. As we proceed through what I hope (and thankfully, think) will be a relatively short dark age of pro-censorship rhetoric, we see advertisers, politicians, and moralists all attempting to "protect" people by dumbing down discourse- this was done in the past with books, didn't work, led to a sort of miniaturized and prolonged cultural revolution, and eventually the rise of the late pre-modern period with its complete overhaul of academia (mostly not for the better, over the last twenty years.)

The internet is the great equalizer and should be seen and referred to as such; so long as it is uncensored it is basically a meritocracy that rewards people who are interesting, compelling, and intelligent. In such a de facto meritocracy (also a technocracy, humorously) the intelligent ultimately have the greatest advantage; they can even outflank the rich for the first time- probably one of the main reasons why the wealthy corporations, dying as they are, are repeatedly doing whatever they can to destroy as much independent content as possible through legalese, censorship, and harassment campaigns which they almost certainly pay to launch on their smaller competitors.

In fact there is no specific single counter-propaganda method I can think of that works as well as simply fielding a completely uncensored internet in which private firms are admonished by population and government alike to simply make their profit and take a hands-off approach to policing websites and such.

INDEPENDENT MEDIA OVER OLD MEDIA, GRASSROOTS OVER ESTABLISHMENT

In closing here one last thing bears mentioning, which is that, usually, it is better to have a decentralized than a centralized situation or, if there must be centrality, it should be limited, reduced, controlled and constrained to a reasonable level. This is the case with most things, but especially with the dissemination of information and political power.

A centralized figure as I have mentioned is no more or less inherently corrupt than someone lacking most power- but they have been given the tools to wreak havoc if they are corrupt, while in a system with far more points of generally far lesser control, such corruption cannot do so much so easily.

The independent media has issues; it can be given over to sensationalism, slander, and unethical reporting. However, is this not just a more minor degree of the same problems we have seen in the old media giants? They have done the same and far worse, from defaming people into an early grave to covering for government lies and corruption. Likewise, grassroots or upstart political fronts can be violent, but the establishment parties, which are supposedly less so, are the ones which control every conflict and start every war. It becomes far harder to control a population which is able to speak freely and at a whim.

At all hazards decentralization should be encouraged and protected.

THE END

www.ingramcontent.com/pod-product-compliance
Lightning Source LLC
Chambersburg PA
CBHW071051260726
48660CB00008B/3166